LAWNS

Mr R. B. Dawson has been Director of the St. Ives
Research Station, Bingley, Yorkshire, since 1929,
when it was founded. This Research Station is maintained by the Sports Turf Research Institute, which
represents the main sporting bodies in this country.
It is a non-profit-making, non-commercial body.
Under Mr Dawson's direction experimental work on
a large scale on all aspects of the management of
grass swards suitable for lawns, greens, football
grounds, playing-fields, etc., is in progress. His
name and that of the Institute are widely known in
Great Britain and on the Continent.
In addition to directing the experimental work, Mr
Dawson is responsible on behalf of the Institute for
maintaining an advisory service to give practical
advice on the needs of turf. Mr Dawson's staff, who
have wide experience on turf problems in all parts
of the country, have collaborated in the preparation
of this book.
Mr Dawson's aim has been to provide the reader
with information which will help him to get good
turf, the aim of the book being the same as that of
the St Ives Research Station, namely to raise the
general standard of turf in this country.

An Amateur Gardening Handbook

THIS BOOK

IS NO 11 OF THE AMATEUR GARDENING HANDBOOKS

others in the series are

NEW TITLES ARE ADDED FROM TIME TO TIME

LAWNS

R. B. DAWSON, M.Sc., F.L.S.

11

W. H. & L. COLLINGRIDGE LTD

2-10 TAVISTOCK STREET COVENT GARDEN LONDON WC2

FIRST PUBLISHED IN 1954

The Amateur Gardening Handbooks
are published by
W. H. & L. Collingridge Limited
2–10 Tavistock Street London WC2
and printed and bound in England by
Hazell Watson & Viney Limited
Aylesbury and London

CONTENTS

ILLUSTRATIONS

BY C. NEWSOME-TAYLOR

6

INTRODUCTION

NEARLY all gardeners and garden lovers appreciate the amenity that a lawn confers upon the home. The lawn can be strictly utilitarian or used to provide contrast to flowers and shrubs, or, again, it can attempt to be both useful and ornamental. The lawn is, in fact, recognized as an essential feature in the vast majority of gardens. It may cover only a few square yards, or it may extend to as much as a quarter of an acre. In some gardens the lawn provides the main feature, with beds and shrubs assuming a very definite second place. Some enthusiasts, indeed, may have a few flowers only to set off the lawn! In other cases the lawn is small and insignificant. No matter what its status, however, the lawn should be designed to make its own contribution to the value of the garden.

Care is needed in planning flower-beds, shrubs and trees within and round the lawn area. Small rectangular or circular beds which 'cut up' the turf area cause a loss of effect. They tend to make the lawn look smaller than it is, while they also introduce problems of maintenance. A bold, striking effect is desirable. If the emphasis of the garden is to be on bedding or borders, let these dominate the lay-out, keeping the lawn as an obvious secondary feature used purely for the purpose of contrast or perhaps as a means of access to parts of the garden.

The shape and contour of the lawn is, of course, influenced by that of the site as well as fixed points, such as the front door, the level of paths, existing trees or perhaps outcrops of rock. Joining such fixed points by a lawn must be done with some skill in order to give a happy result. The owner may have to make up his mind as to whether he wants a pleasing view from the window or whether he wishes to convey a good impression to the visitor as he enters the garden. It may be possible, if space permits, to satisfy both conditions, though of course there will be many instances where the lawn is solely a 'utility' model.

There is no need for a lawn to be horizontal, but it must be smooth enough for proper mowing. It can be terraced or undulating, but all ridges and slopes must be gradual so that mowing is facilitated, while water-holding depressions or pockets must be avoided. Hard-and-fast rules as to lay-out cannot be determined; so much depends on the aspirations of the owner, the nature of the site and its surroundings.

Unfortunately, present-day housing estates do not permit much latitude in planning a garden, let alone a lawn. There may seem little option but to provide an oblong or square piece of turf on a fairly flat site covering perhaps 50 or even up to 200 square yards in all and surrounded by narrow borders. This is not necessary, but how often does one see row after row of them? The established lawn could be modified, and certainly there is no need for the new one to be planned on such ordinary lines. By using some ingenuity and imagination, an irregular shape can be planned with borders of varying width, thus providing a curving edge instead of a straight one. Some undulations, a terrace, a break with shrubs, can all be considered, while the turf can be made to merge into or combine with a rock garden, a crazy-paving path, steps or a sunken garden or other features.

Of course, where the house is detached there is usually much more scope to enable a more attractive lay-out, perhaps with banks and with verges designed to lead the eye to the main garden features. There is much to be said for not disclosing all the features of the garden at once—there should be some element of surprise.

No matter what the lay-out of the lawn, it cannot be good unless it has some care and attention expended upon it. Unfortunately, many people, though convinced of the need for good treatment of flowers and vegetables, fail to take positive steps to get a good turf on the lawn. 'Oh, it's only grass,' they say as they take another cut off with the mower, 'let's hope it won't need cutting again for some time.' It is all a question of standard; the higher the requirement the more careful must be the work, because a good turf is as much a crop as our flowers or vegetables, but with the disadvantage that the crop gets walked upon!

Something should be said about the qualities of a good lawn and the objectives. First of all, it should provide good, even colour with uniformity of texture. Most people prefer to see turf that is weed-free, and of course no one wants diseases and pests. A true surface, meaning one that is free from sharp lumps and hollows, is neces-sary because this permits the mower to flow over the surface evenly, so giving a uniform cut. The turf of the ideal lawn should consist of dwarf grasses capable of standing up to regular close mowing. Where the lawn is utilitarian, it should be tough enough to resist wear and tear. The turf should be reasonably drought resistant yet not subject to water-logging. Edges should be neatly trimmed, and mowing carried out regularly in such a way as to give a neat and tidy pattern.

Producing a first-class lawn is not easy, and the purpose of this book is to outline the general principles of good lawn craft in simple terms. It is primarily intended for owners of relatively small lawns, the men (and women) who do the work themselves, and may thus need simple practical guidance for personal use. This book also aims to help the gardener to recognize faults and to apply the right remedies. In short, the aim is to raise the standard of the domestic lawn, which unfortunately too often occupies a low level. While the owner seldom requires a turf up to the standard needed on a first-class golf- or bowling-green, he will get immense personal satisfaction and pleasure from his own efforts in getting the turf into good order. It can become the envy of the neighbours and lead to much friendly rivalry—perhaps some day we shall see competitions run by horticultural societies to find the best lawn in the district! This would at least stimulate interest in what can prove a very absorbing subject for the gardener prepared to go to a little extra trouble, use common sense and pay careful attention to detail. Readers who desire a more comprehensive treatise on the subject of lawns are referred to the author's book *Practical Lawn Craft* (Crosby, Lockwood).

Part One: New Lawns

CHAPTER ONE

PREPARING THE SITE

THE house owner who finds the site of his new lawn in such a state that little constructional work is necessary is indeed fortunate. Where the house is newly built the garden area is often partially covered with builder's debris, while sub-soil may have been deposited on the vacant ground during the process of excavating the house foundations. Unsuitable material must be removed before work can start. If, on the other hand, the site is covered with undisturbed pasture-land turf of reasonable quality, it may be possible to work this up by degrees into a ready-made lawn. It might prove necessary, of course, first to strip off the turf, shape the ground below to the desired contours, and then relay (see Chapter Five).

If a new lawn is to be established in the course of replanning the garden, the work entailed in the initial preparation may not be great, especially if the site was formerly used for vegetable growing or bedding.

First Steps Assuming the site has been cleaned or the existing turf removed and no special treatment, e.g. grading of the surface or drainage is necessary, thorough digging should be the first job. Bastard trenching two spits deep is recommended for sites where the soil has been compacted through traffic during building operations, the method being illustrated in Fig. 1. The first

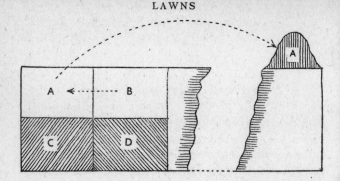

1. *In bastard trenching, the soil is worked to a depth of two spits.*

spit (A) is removed to form a trench and the soil transported to the far end of the site. (C) is then forked and (B) is then turned over on to (A). The bottom of the trench formed is broken up (D). This procedure is followed until the whole site has been treated, the last open trench being filled with the soil removed to form the trench (A) at the start.

Usually, however, straight digging (Fig. 2) will be sufficient. If there is a rough grass cover, the old sod should be well buried, while on previously cultivated land annual weeds should be buried and obnoxious perennials such as dandelion, docks and couch, removed. This work is best carried out during the late autumn months, the ground being left in a rough state to weather during the winter.

Grading the Site The levels of every lawn are likely to be governed by such fixed points as the damp-course of the house or the footpaths but it may be necessary to

2. Plain digging should be carried out methodically, working backwards across the plot.

alter the existing contours of the ground in order to tie these together or to form a pleasing but practical surface. Where the land has a slope a terraced lawn may find favour, in which case 'cut-and-fill' (Fig. 3) construction will be required. A gentle slope is not necessarily a bad thing, since there is no need, usually, for the lawn to be exactly in a horizontal plane, but if the slope is too marked, grading is probably called for. A slightly undulating surface may prove attractive and suitable in some situations.

When levels need to be altered, there is, of course, more than one way of arriving at a satisfactory final position. Where minor changes are involved these can be effected by raking the soil from higher to lower places, provided that care is taken to leave not less than 4 to 6 in. of good top-spit soil. Obviously the procedure is limited in its application by this requirement, and a more fundamental approach may be necessary. The simple way is often the acquisition of a load or two of top-soil, which can be spread out as required. The alternative is to remove the top-soil temporarily to one side and adjust the levels in the sub-soil before replacing the top-soil. The 'cut-and-fill' procedure is again indicated (Fig. 3). Where space is limited, it may be necessary to divide the area into two halves by a line in the direction of the slope so that the top-soil from one half can be placed on the other half while the first half is being graded and vice versa. In making a terraced lawn similar considerations apply, special care being required with the banks. At the completion of the constructional work involved in adjusting levels, top-soil is spread evenly over the area to give a final depth of top spit of 4 to 6 in.

In grading work on small lawns the average householder will be satisfied that he can judge his levels sufficiently accurately by eye or with the aid of a string or two. For the fastidious, or where bigger projects make this unreliable, the following procedure is recommended.

First choose a datum point and drive in firmly a large flat-topped peg, leaving it, say, 4 in. above the soil surface. Further similar pegs should be inserted at measured dis-

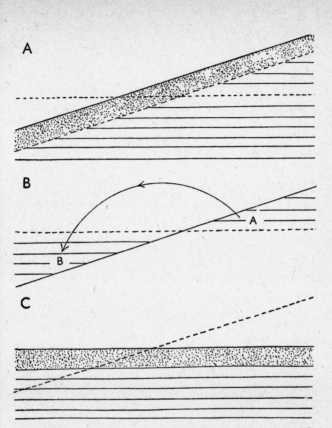

3. *Grading a site by the 'cut-and-fill' method. (A) The dotted line represents the proposed level. The shaded portion is the good top-soil; this is removed (B) and the site levelled. The top-soil is then returned (C).*

tance from this in lines and cross lines. These pegs should be set to a true level, using a straight-edge and spirit-level. Where a horizontal surface is required, the soil (or sub-soil) should be worked to a definite position down the pegs. On the other hand, where a slope is wanted blocks should be added to the tops of the pegs as appropriate, and the earth worked to a definite position relative to the new peg tops. In the procedure just described the eye is still used to estimate the height from the top of the peg to the soil, and some people find the use of string a great help. In working to produce a slight slope, thoughtful use of strings may dispense with the need for blocks after a datum level has been obtained with the straight-edge and spirit-level.

Constructional work is best carried out during the dry summer weather to avoid damaging the soil. The land can then be dug over and left in a fairly rough state for the winter. Any bulky soil ameliorants, such as manure or compost, as well as lime if necessary, may be worked in during the digging.

Drainage On most small lawns the trouble of draining is scarcely justified, but where conditions are wet a single 3-in. pipe leading to a disposal point, such as a sump or soak-away, should be adequate. On very large lawns on wet land a properly planned drainage system may be required. Where drainage is likely to be necessary it may be installed during constructional work, or it may be left over for a year or two to see how the lawn behaves without it. Suitable drainage systems for lawns are also discussed in Chapter Fourteen.

Banks   There are two important points to watch when making a bank. Firstly, it must have a proper covering of top-soil just as other parts of the lawn, and this should be not less than 4 in. thick, but 6 in. is better. Secondly, the angle of slope must not be more than 30°—it can be less to advantage, but should certainly be no more. Steep banks are difficult to mow, especially if high, and, moreover, establishing seed upon them is not easy. If turfed, the sods have to be pegged down until rooted. South-facing banks, especially steep ones, are hard to keep decent in dry weather. Often the turf dies, thus weakening the surface and perhaps permitting weed to enter.

CHAPTER TWO

PREPARING THE FINAL SOIL-BED

AFTER digging, the final preparation of the soil-bed is very similar whether the lawn is to be established from seed or from turf, though the final bed for seeding needs to be rather better than for turfing. The object is to produce to the required contours an evenly firmed, true surface surmounted by a thin mulch of fine earth into which the seed is to be sown or upon which the turf is to be laid. The thoroughness with which this work is carried out will be reflected for a long time after the lawn is established, and therefore great pains should be taken to do the work correctly. Rolling, illustrated in Fig. 4, A, is designed to break down the larger clods of soil; while heeling (Fig. 4, B) is the most satisfactory method of ensuring the surface is evenly firmed. Raking (Fig. 4, C) fines down the soil and ensures the production of a true surface, free from large stones.

In the first instance alternate rolling and cultivating with the Canterbury hoe or cultivator (Fig. 4, D) should be practised until a reasonably fine tilth exists and the surface has been firmed a little. When this has been achieved, further raking in conjunction with heeling is necessary until all local soft spots have been firmed and the degree of compaction is uniform over the whole surface. In carrying out the work, one must continually endeavour to produce a true surface. Small bumps or

18

4. *Soil preparation.* (*A*) *Rolling.* (*B*) *Heeling.* (*C*) *Raking.*
(*D*) *A 5-tined cultivator used for breaking up the soil to
produce a fine tilth.*

19

hollows resulting from poor raking or uneven sinkage create difficulties in maintenance at a later date.

Improving the Nature of the Soil Though grass swards will grow in a very wide range of conditions, it is often necessary and desirable to improve the quality of the soil to get really good results. Heavy soils have a tendency to hold too much moisture, and may be lightened with advantage. The addition of coarse, gritty sand at a rate of some 7 to 14 lb. per square yard may be satisfactory, but no doubt the quantity used will be governed by its cost. Fine clinker ash or coke breeze serve as suitable substitutes. Peat, well-decomposed farmyard manure or other similar organic matter also prove of value, especially on the light, sandy soils where increased moisture-holding capacity is required. Rates of application of peat are dependent on the soil type, but 4 to 7 lb. per square yard is quite usual. Well-rotted farmyard manure being heavier does not go so far as the equivalent weight of peat, and some 7 to 10 lb. should be used.

The application of such materials should be made as soon as possible after final grading has been completed to get them thoroughly and uniformly worked into the top-spit soil. They may be incorporated during the digging or forked in later.

Lime It is mentioned elsewhere (Chapter Ten), that the fine and most suitable grasses for garden lawns thrive in a slightly acid soil. Should the soil on the new lawn site be found very acid, however, a corrective lime dressing should be made. A garden soil which has grown good vegetable crops is not usually deficient in lime, whereas if the site was originally covered with turf of a very fibrous nature, this is a good indication that the soil is acid. Ground carbonate of lime, also called ground limestone, is the most suitable form of lime to use, the rate of application to correct over-acid conditions being usually in the region of 2 to 4 oz. per square yard. If lime is required, it should be applied in the early stages of cultivation.

Fertilizer Treatment Much depends on the previous history of the land. Where vegetables have been grown, the chances are that fertilizer treatment is superfluous or even harmful. If the land is not very rich, however, then a suitable pretreatment is advantageous when the lawn is to be sown. This may take the form of a complete garden fertilizer, but a special mix for lawn purposes may be made up as follows: $\frac{1}{2}$ oz. of sulphate of ammonia, 1 oz. of superphosphate, 1 oz. of bonemeal, $\frac{1}{4}$ oz. of sulphate of potash. The quantities given are per square yard and the fertilizer should be applied evenly 7 to 10 days before the grass seed and well raked in.

When turfing, it is usual, because of the time of the year, to omit the sulphate of ammonia from the above mixture, and, in fact, many people content themselves with a dressing of bonemeal or superphosphate, and then follow up with a complete dressing in the spring.

Timing of Operations and Fallowing Turf should be laid in autumn and early winter, while grass seed may be sown either in the spring or, better, in the late summer. It is necessary to take these facts into account in planning the various operations leading up to them. When constructional work takes place in the summer, the land will not be fit for sowing down the same season, but may be by the following spring. On the other hand, turfing, which does not require quite such good conditions and comes later on, may be done at the end of the first season. Whether one is sowing or turfing, however, there is much to be said for allowing a full summer's fallowing, at the end of which the land can be sown or turfed. Where constructional work is not required, it is easier to plan for suitable fallowing, without which the quality of the lawn is likely to leave much to be desired.

Fallowing is directed primarily at producing a soil-bed free from weeds. Ideally the work entailed should start in the spring, and should be continued until early August, the area treated being several inches larger than the dimensions of the final lawn. Periodic raking and cultivating with a Canterbury hoe or cultivator (Fig. 4, D) should be undertaken as the development of weed species is noticed. Under no circumstances should any weed be allowed to reach the flowering stage before it is destroyed; in fact, the more the soil can be worked the greater the chance of eliminating the largest number of weeds. It should be remembered in carrying out this work that a good opportunity for working down the soil to the final level is provided.

CHAPTER THREE

SEED OR TURF?

A DECISION must first of all be made as to whether the
new lawn is to be sown or turfed. There is no doubt that
given a good seed-bed and a suitable mixture, seeding
is the more reliable method of establishment for a fine-
textured lawn. The cost is also less. The disadvantages of
seeding, as against turfing, are that a very fine, clean seed-
bed must be obtained, especially for the finest grass seeds;
a certain amount of seed may be lost to birds, and seedling
grasses are rather more susceptible to adverse weather
conditions and disease. The difficulty with turfing lies
primarily in obtaining suitable material. Even when a
fairly good supply is chanced upon, there is likely to be
quite considerable variability as between the separate
sods.

Seed Mixtures It is first necessary to decide whether a
strictly ornamental lawn of the finest texture is wanted
or whether the lawn is to act as a general playground.
For the best type of ornamental lawn fescue and bent
seeds should be chosen and a mixture of 80% Chewing's
fescue and 20% New Zealand browntop bent will be
found to give every satisfaction on a well-prepared soil.
A slightly cheaper but coarser, hard-wearing turf (though
still without rye-grass) will be provided by a mixture of:
55% Chewing's fescue, 35% crested dog's-tail, 10% New
Zealand browntop bent; while those wanting a relatively

cheap seed mixture which will produce a very durable hard-wearing turf may use something like: 45% Chewing's fescue or S.59 creeping red fescue, 25% perennial rye-grass, 20% crested dog's-tail, 7% rough-stalked meadow grass, 3% New Zealand browntop bent. This rye-grass mixture, however, would by no means suit the connoisseur requiring a really fine lawn. Many gardeners will go to one of the multiple stores for a cheap mixture. Although good value may be obtained, a cheap mixture cannot give a first-class lawn.

Turf For the turfed lawn you must (with apologies to Mrs. Beeton) 'first find your turf'. It is unlikely that turf of fine uniform texture will be found unless sea-marsh turf is used, and this is not a practice generally to be recommended. Turf of this type is derived from coastal marshes, and when laid in the average garden, where conditions are not ideal for its growth, requires very skilful management if it is not to deteriorate rapidly. Turf composed of a mixture of fescue and bent is at times obtainable from hillsides and neglected upland pastures. These fine grasses persist under poor soil conditions, and are kept short by grazing. Unfortunately such turf usually has a thick layer of fibre, as a result of which it is slow to root down and become well established. Provided the turf is lifted thin, watered in dry weather and given time, a valuable sward can be produced. Old parkland turf is sometimes offered, and so long as it is not too fibrous it can give good results in its new home.

No matter what turf is chosen, it should contain a proportion of fescue and bent. It should not contain too much fibre, while all turves containing much coarse grass, such as cock's-foot, Yorkshire fog or creeping soft grass, should be discarded. Turf selected should be as free from weed as possible. Traces of clover are not always easy to spot. This weed is relatively hard to eradicate, and if in new turf can cause trouble the year after laying. Small

5. *The turf is cut cleanly with a half-moon cutter or edging-iron (A) and lifted with a turf-float (B).*

pieces of undesirable grass and weeds can be hand-picked out of the sods before laying is done.

Sometimes the gardener can find a source of turf in the immediate neighbourhood if he lives on the outskirts of a town. This may permit personal inspection, as against buying from a supplier many miles away. He may have to lift the turf himself, and the following brief description of the method of lifting turf may therefore be helpful. Figure 5, A, illustrates the use of the edging-iron or half-moon cutter. The turf is first of all nicked vertically in 1-ft. wide strips, and the amateur will probably find it easiest to intersect these lines by cross cuts at 1-ft. intervals so that 1 ft. × 1 ft. turves result. A line must be used for this work. In the trade the turf is usually lifted in 3 ft. × 1 ft. rectangles, which can be rolled. An implement known as a 'turf-float' is used (see Fig. 5, B). A piece of turf must be removed at the end of each strip in order that the float can be pushed in below the turf. The head of the float should be kept in a horizontal position so that the thickness of the turves is uniform—not thin at one end and thick at the other. A common thickness is 1½ in. In the absence of a float, a spade with a good, long, wide, straight blade may be used, but this is more laborious and more care has to be exercised. Indeed, turf so lifted may well have to be boxed to uniform thickness (see Chapter Five).

CHAPTER FOUR

ESTABLISHMENT BY SEEDING

Which is the Best Time to Sow? It will be appreciated that where extensive preparation of the lawn site is necessary to ensure the production of a clean seed-bed to the desired contours, sowing is best carried out during August, or perhaps early September in warm districts. Where, however, the site has been frequently cultivated, a late spring sowing may be possible, but experience shows that the young grass plants are at times jeopardized.

Young swards produced from a spring sowing may have to face periods of dry weather and hot sun. This can seriously retard the young plants. If a long drought develops and artificial water is not permitted, many grass plants will die. Further, artificial water never seems so effective as rain, and the spray used may even knock plants out of the ground or expose their roots.

The aim with new lawns should be rapid establishment with maximum density as quickly as possible. In dry conditions this is unlikely. Moreover, if the soil was not fallowed or cleaned effectively, competition offered by weed species, especially annuals such as chickweed and groundsel and the usually biennial shepherd's-purse, is increased. Their presence is a great threat to the density of the grass cover that one is trying to produce.

By sowing in late August or early September these dangers are greatly reduced. There is a longer period of favourable weather in which to prepare the land while the germination of grass seed is favoured by soil warmth and moister atmospheric conditions. An August sowing gives the young seedlings ample opportunity to become established before the onset of wintry weather.

Sowing   The need for the production of a fine tilth has been discussed, and if the seed mixture to be used is composed of the fine grass species fescue and bent, this is particularly important. In any case, the soil should be dry and the surface should be given a final light raking before sowing. The opportunity, the last before the lawn is established, should be taken to correct any remaining unevenness.

Quantity of Seed   All is now set for distributing the seed, and this is most satisfactorily done by hand. The seeds mixture for the finest textured sward, i.e. Chewing's fescue and New Zealand browntop (see Chapter Three) should be sown at a total rate of 1½ oz. per square yard. This is admittedly a substantial rate for seed that will cost from 7s. 6d. to 8s. 6d. per pound. It can be reduced, provided time is spent on producing a fine, clean seed-bed, pretreating with fertilizer and timing operations for sowing the seed in, say, mid-August. Using seed of good viability and observing the points above, rates of 1 oz. per square yard or even ¾ oz. are quite adequate.

Using a fescue/bent mixture, it is quite a good plan to sow each species separately, which means, of course, they must be bought separately. The fescue, being the larger seed, should be sown first, then lightly raked in. Seed of bent is very small, and so it should be broadcast on to the raked surface and then only very lightly worked in. A dry sack pulled over the area will do this ideally.

For the New Zealand browntop, Chewing's fescue and crested dog's-tail mixture, the total rate of sowing should be 1 oz. per square yard, but where the mixture containing rye-grass is used, the rate can be reduced to $\frac{3}{4}$ oz. or even $\frac{1}{2}$ oz. per square yard. Lower rates are possible under ideal conditions with both the above.

How to Sow The total quantity of seed required should be divided in half, the portions being sown separately in opposite directions. If this is done, the seed is likely to be applied more evenly. The importance of this must be fully appreciated. Thus, when germination takes place, the young seedlings being evenly spaced, do not crowd each other too badly and, further, there is no variation in density. Such a cover offers greater competition against the establishment of weed species.

Should it be felt that an even sowing over the area cannot be achieved with confidence even after dividing the seed into two lots, the site should be strung off into squares. The need should then be divided into small lots equalling double the number of squares, each square then being sown in cross directions (Fig. 6). To assist one in improving the chances of evenly sowing the seed, a quantity of dry, finely screened soil or sharp, dry sand may be mixed with the seed, e.g. if the rate of sowing is $\frac{3}{4}$ oz. per square yard, four times as much sand should be thoroughly mixed with the seed, the mixture then being sown at a rate of $3\frac{3}{4}$ oz. per square yard.

Raking In and Rolling Except when sowing fescue and

bent separately, as described above, the first job after sowing is to rake in. It must be done lightly so that the seed is not buried deeply—it must be only just below the surface. The sown area should be lightly and gently raked (Fig. 6), in a direction transverse to the last raking done before sowing. Bent seed especially does not like

6. *Divide the site into equal sections before sowing (left); sow broadcast fashion, then rake the seed in (right).*

being buried too deeply, hence the special method of sowing described earlier on.

While it is quite common to put a light roller over the surface following the raking to firm up the soil round the seeds, there are sound arguments against this. For instance, where a fine seed-bed is made on medium to heavy land, rolling can result in greater caking of the surface after rain. This cake interferes with establishment. On light soils a rolled surface is apt to 'blow away', taking the seed along, too, more readily than a surface left slightly rougher. An unrolled surface, besides reducing risk of wind loss, does help a little to shield the seedlings. Light rolling is, of course, a wise practice once the seedlings have germinated and are about 1 in. long.

On town lawns birds, principally house sparrows, can be a serious nuisance on a newly sown lawn. It is not so much the grass seeds they eat as their habit of dust-bathing, and so badly upsetting the surface. The answer is a few strands of black cotton supported on short sticks 2 or 3 in. above the surface.

CHAPTER FIVE

ESTABLISHMENT BY TURFING

The Season for Turfing If a satisfactory establishment from turf is to be achieved, it is best to carry out the work during the late autumn and early winter months. The advantage is that the turf will be settled in position by the early spring, and the new roots produced will hasten its establishment into the underlying soil. This point is important, as turf laid in March has often not rooted down before dry periods of weather are experienced. Shrinkage may then result in gaps between the turves, and even cause death along the edges. Drying out caused by sun and wind causes a general check to establishment.

Turfing during the period December to February is, of course, a possibility if the intermittent periods of really bad weather can be avoided; but soil conditions are still such that there may be difficulty in working it correctly. This means the turf may be laid on very lumpy or muddy soil.

A further point to be borne in mind is that there should be minimum delay between lifting and relaying the turf. It is often necessary to store it for a time—in stacks if space is limited. If left for more than a few days in this condition it suffers a severe set-back—the grass goes yellow, starts to decay, and when finally laid, apart from suffering a check, will be prone to disease, e.g. fusarium patch disease. If laying is delayed, the turf is best spread out flat near where it is to be used. In this position little harm will result even if periods of frost and snow intervene.

Boxing Turf The determined efforts made to produce a true surface on which to lay the turf are nullified if the turf used has not been cut to uniform thickness. Should this be so, it will be well worth-while boxing the turf before laying. The operation is illustrated in Fig. 7, A. The box is in a sense an open-ended tray into which the turf is laid grass face down. The depth of the tray decides the thickness of the turf. If the box is 2 in. deep and $1\frac{1}{2}$-in. thick turf is wanted, then pack with $\frac{1}{2}$-in. boards. A stout knife is drawn across the top edges of the box, thus slicing the turf to a uniform depth. An old scythe blade can be used if hand grips are made from pieces of sacking. The amateur may be forced to use a spade or edging-iron.

Laying the Turf The soil surface should be prepared as for seeding, but the need for obtaining as fine a tilth is not so great. Turfing should start at one side or corner of the site, the turves being laid across the area. Those which

7. *Boxing the turf to reduce it to uniform thickness (A) before laying it (B).*

form the actual lawn edge should be laid some 3 in. in from the edge of the prepared soil surface to ensure that they are actually situated on a firm bed. Laying should be carried out in a forward direction, i.e. the person laying should face the unturfed soil and should be actually walking on the area he has just laid. Fig. 7, B, illustrates the method, and it should be noticed that planks are placed on the newly laid turf to prevent the formation of foot-marks and disturbance. If it is necessary to barrow the supply of turf on to the site, planks should be laid down for the wheel to run on. Again, this point is important if the efforts to produce a true surface are not to be nullified.

All turf must be laid as neatly as possible, the turves being bonded like the bricks in a wall. No space should be left at the joints, the turves being packed tightly together. The surface produced should be true. This will come more or less naturally if the surface has been well prepared and the turf cut to a uniform thickness. Should a corner or a side of a turf be low, packing underneath with fine soil to correct it is all that is necessary. Beating the turves to produce a true surface should be unnecessary and can be very detrimental.

Uniform turves laid neatly together on a true soil surface will only require light rolling at intervals to encourage settling down and root hold.

Top-dressing When laying has been completed any obvious open joints should be filled with finely screened top-dressing. The whole area should then receive a general top-dressing (see Chapter Seven).

CHAPTER SIX

UNORTHODOX WAYS OF MAKING
A LAWN

In addition to producing lawns by sowing or turfing or by working down an existing meadow or pasture turf, they can be established by a still further method known as the vegetative process. This method is common in tropical or semi-tropical countries, using Bermuda grass, and much turf has also been made in this way in the United States with runners or stolons from bents with a creeping habit of growth. In the United States stolons grown from recognized strains of creeping bent are commercially available, but this is not so in Great Britain. Therefore to make a vegetative lawn it would first be necessary to grow a crop of such runners using a leafy strain of creeping bent (*Agrostis stolonifera*) or a suitable type of velvet bent (*A. canina*). The runners grown on the crowns of the plant are pulled off the parent, cut into lengths 2 to 3 in. long and scattered over a soil-bed prepared as for seeding. One square foot of stolons will make 9 or 10 square feet of lawn. No soil space should be left greater than 1 square inch and a thin cover of soil and a light rolling should follow. July or early August are good times to do the planting. If kept moist, roots and shoots are soon produced at the nodes on the chopped-up runners and by degrees under careful mowing and top-dressing the young plants bunch out and eventually join up. Unwanted weeds and weed grasses must be hand-picked from among the young bent grass.

Another way is to tear up a piece of turf of one of the bent grasses. Creeping bent or velvet bent, as well as browntop (*Agrostis tenuis*), can all be used. Velvet bent produces a dense cover of fine-leaved grass having good colour, and connoisseurs have described it as the queen of lawn grasses. Small bundles of shoots about the thickness of a pencil are planted on the prepared soil bed at 2- to 3-in. intervals. The bundles of shoots soon root down, begin to bunch out, and eventually join up to make a continuous cover, provided, of course, careful mowing, light feeding and top-dressing are carried out. The top-dressing is most important to get satisfactory spread of the grasses in either of the above methods.

These vegetative methods of making turf are very interesting, but take longer than seeding or turfing, especially when a crop of stolons has first to be grown. Few gardeners will have the time and the space to undertake such projects.

Chamomile   Some mention must be made of chamomile lawns, about which there have been frequent references in gardening papers. A lawn solely composed of the plant is not really practicable. The most that can be hoped for is a grass lawn in which are growing fairly frequent patches of the plant. The species to use is *Anthemis nobilis,* and here again the gardener must propagate his own material. Plants grown in a bed produce many side-shoots sprawling on the surface. These can be broken off, struck as cuttings, and then transplanted. If making a new lawn, a good plan is to sow grass seed in the ordinary way, and when the seedlings are well through to set in small transplanted seedlings of chamomile every 9 to 12 in.

A lawn containing chamomile must not be cut too keenly, and rather more rolling may be needed than is normally good for grass. Of course selective weed-killers used to control weed would seriously affect if not destroy the chamomile. When established in the lawn, the chamomile emits a very pleasant aroma when walked upon.

In New Zealand lawns and greens are sometimes made with species of *Cotula,* and more recently a species of *Sagina* has been suggested as having possibilities.

As a final word on unorthodox procedure, many lawn owners try to patch up bare places in the sward by putting in plants of grasses dug up on paths and flower-beds. This is a dangerous practice, since the wrong species can easily be used unless the owner can identify his grasses. Plants of browntop (*Agrostis tenuis*) are satisfactory, but the amateur is much more likely to get hold of annual meadow grass.

CHAPTER SEVEN

AFTER-CARE OF THE NEW LAWN

MANY a promising new lawn has been spoilt by lack of attention in the vital few months immediately following sowing seed or laying turf. Naturally enough, the after-care of a seeded lawn differs somewhat from that of a lawn established by turf.

Seeded Lawns After sowing the lawn, a close watch should be kept on the developing seedlings. There is a disease known as 'damping off' that is liable to affect seedling grass, particularly if the seed was sown thickly. A number of common fungi can cause the trouble. The disease is less likely to attack new grass if care was taken to buy and sow good-quality seed and if a good, dry seed-bed was obtained ready for the sowing. The disease appears first as small bronze patches, but later the affected foliage topples over to form a rotten mass. If such dis-coloration is noticed, no time should be lost in carrying out control measures using a solution of Cheshunt compound. The rate is $\frac{1}{2}$ oz. dissolved in 1 gallon of water to each square yard. If the young grass appears to be weak and of poor colour, a dressing of sulphate of ammonia at the rate of $\frac{1}{2}$ oz. per square yard may be beneficial, especially if sowing was done in spring. It must not be given unless bulked with a carrier or made into a very weak solution.

All being well, some four to six weeks after sowing the

new grass will come in for the first mowing. It should be about 1½ in. long when this is done. A side-wheel machine with the sole plate set high is best, for only the tips of the leaves are removed. It is usually necessary to give a light roll before this first mowing to firm the soil round the grass plants, but such rolling should only be done in dry weather. A single mowing may be sufficient for that year if sowing was done in August/September, but after a spring sowing naturally the mower will be in action regularly, the height of cut being reduced gradually in successive mowings until normal height of cut is achieved.

A few annual weeds will probably appear, such as chickweed, groundsel or fat-hen, but there should not be many if the fallowing process before sowing was properly carried out. Isolated annual weeds which do appear with the new grass will be killed during the process of regular mowing. In addition, and this is much more serious, certain weed grasses are likely to appear. If for example a sowing of fescue and bent was made then plants of perennial rye-grass, crested dog's tail or rough-stalked meadow grass found in it can rightly be regarded as weed grasses and they should be removed. They are, of course, ingredients of less expensive seed mixtures but undesirable impurities in a first-class fine turf. Other grasses to remove are annual meadow grass, Yorkshire fog and creeping soft grass—the last two being best taken out of all lawn sowings whatever the quality of seed mixture sown. Some of these grasses may have come as impurities in the original seeds mixture, while seeds of annual meadow grass will probably have been present in the soil, since the grass is ubiquitous. The only method of removing these is old-fashioned hand weeding! Unless these coarse grasses are removed as seedlings they can make much work and unsightliness later on. The new lawn must be gone over carefully, picking out all these coarser grasses which will stand out conspicuously in the future lawn. With a large lawn it is best to string out in yard strips and hand weed one strip at a time.

About eight weeks after the sowing of the seed, it will be time to give a top-dressing of about 4 lb. to the square yard of friable, dry, screened compost or an appropriate substitute. The application should be made under dry conditions, and to prevent smothering of the grass sward it should be well worked in with a drag-mat. There may be certain places in the lawn where the original seeding has failed, and these should be resown eventually when the time is ripe (a lawn sown in spring should be renovated at the end of the summer). The same seed mixture as was originally sown should, of course, be used for renovation. During dry spells of weather following a spring sowing, it is important that artificial watering should be done.

It will be remembered that in establishing a lawn by seed, a margin some 3 in. wide round the site of the future lawn was also treated and sown. When the lawn is firmly established, perhaps by late summer, this 3-in. fringe should be trimmed off with a half-moon cutter at a slight angle in the first instance, and later, as the root system increases, it can be made vertical.

Turfed Lawns   The first thing to be done after the laying

40

of a turfed lawn is to get on a top-dressing for the purpose of filling in the joints between the turves and truing up the surface. A fairly generous dressing of fine compost or a soil/sand mixture may be applied at the rate of 4 to 7 lb. per square yard, and should be worked into the joins and the surface of the turf by a drag-mat. Whatever is given must be light and sandy; indeed, on heavier soils sand only can be used. It may be necessary to give one or two repeat applications of this top-dressing during the autumn and winter following the laying of the lawn. The amount and frequency of the dressing depends on the trueness of the surface produced when laying the turf.

Since turf is best laid in the autumn or early winter, it is unlikely that much mowing will be required until the spring, but the grass should not be allowed to grow too high. No matter what their origin, sods are never of uniform quality, and it may be that one or two will fail to establish. It should be possible to pick these out after the new lawn has been down for three months, and any such poor turves should be replaced during the later part of winter.

Provided the soil was pretreated before laying the turf, no other fertilizer should be needed till spring. A general fertilizer, or at least a nitrogenous one, will then be required in order to encourage the further development of the turf. Following application of this fertilizer any small bare or exceptionally thin places should be renovated with seed.

It is common to find on turfed lawns that there is a fibrous 'mat' close to the surface. This must be reduced by regular wire-raking, which must not be too drastic. The raking will also help to fine down the turf and reduce the amount of coarse grass in it. Raking in the spring can be fairly vigorous, but after that only light, periodic rakings should be done during the rest of the growing season. Naturally the edges of the newly turfed lawn should be trimmed once the turf has got a thorough hold on the soil.

Part Two: Existing Lawns

CHAPTER EIGHT

COMMON TROUBLES

MANY of the trials and tribulations experienced on the established lawn can be traced back to a bad start, or simply to years of neglect or ill-treatment. The effects of hasty site construction, or sowing the wrong sort of seed mixture or sowing incorrectly can easily result in early setbacks. If the lawn has been made of poor or badly laid turf, it may also be hard to get the desired results. Laying aside the faults of relatively new turf, many well-defined troubles also occur on the old-established lawn. Perhaps sheer neglect, failure to follow any proper plan or do anything at all must be mentioned as the first cause.

Incorrect Mowing   Mowing is often done badly, mostly irregularly and usually too closely. Close mowing soon leads to thinness, and may favour the entry of weeds able to grow in spite of the mowing. Clover, pearlwort and moss are a few worthy of special mention in this connexion. Irregular mowing in which the lawn is allowed to grow long and then mowed down hard weakens the grass and can only lead to poor results. A badly shaped lawn with sharp angles and overhanging plants is a trouble in itself because it is tiresome to mow.

Soil Surface   A deficiency of actual top-soil leads to perennial trouble, while subsoil on or near the surface means poor turf. Badly carried-out 'cut-and-fill' construction is sometimes a cause of this.

A surface made muddy by earthworm casts will never produce a good turf in the accepted sense. The earthworms must be removed. Don't forget that a muddy turf is nearly always weedy, and furthermore the constant production of casts causes a loss of trueness and thus accurate mowing becomes impossible. Most gardeners are rather fond of earthworms but in lawns their disadvantages certainly outweigh any possible advantages.

Moisture   A properly cultivated lawn cannot be obtained where the soil is water-logged, and on very heavy soils poor results are likely unless the soil can be opened up and lightened by sand or other gritty matter. At the other end of the scale, lawns on light, sandy or sometimes chalky soils can be very difficult in drought. Artificial watering may be needed to prevent death of some areas; for example, on south-facing banks.

Acidity   Some old lawns suffer from an accumulation of surface fibre or what is known as 'mat'. When a lawn becomes very matted in this way, it is more susceptible to drought and is much slower to recover when the rain falls. Usually this accumulation is due to the soil surface being acid, and while some degree of acidity is desirable, it can be overdone and the layer of mat can become too great. The process is often accelerated in areas subject to atmospheric pollution, since mineral acids reach the turf from the atmosphere. The condition can be relieved by scarification and by hollow forking, but sometimes it is necessary to lime lightly. Care is needed not to give too much. Often very matted lawns are also deficient in plant foods, and fertilizer treatment is necessary in addition.

Usage Perhaps wear and tear is one of the most serious problems the householder is up against when trying to produce a good garden lawn. Children can hardly be denied use of the lawn, but everyone with a family will agree that the damage produced can be very heavy.

It is impossible to get a really first-class effect if the lawn is to be a play-ground. General wear rubs off the grass and muddies the surface, while wheels of cycles and tricycles and so on cause repeated damage. Livestock often make things difficult—it is sometimes impossible to keep a good lawn where there is a bitch, since the urine causes so many brown patches. The family man is therefore likely to find it difficult to have a lawn anything like a bowling green unless he has two lawns—one for the family and one for ornamental purposes! Nevertheless, even the family lawn will be more popular if kept in as good a condition as possible.

Repeated rolling and treading over-compacts the soil, especially if it is of the heavier kind. Grass cannot thrive properly in soil that is too solid, because of the restriction on root development and penetration of moisture and air. This compaction can be relieved by appropriate forking.

Trees Garden lawns often suffer by the close proximity of trees. Roots lying below the turf absorb moisture and plant foods, leading to drying out and poverty. Sometimes the roots come to the surface and interfere with mowing, while shade and constant drip, especially in town areas, can do a lot of harm. Lopping of the boughs should be considered. A good lawn must have plenty of light

45

and air; damp surface conditions under hedges and trees often lead to disease. Lawns, fortunately, are not prone to frequent attacks of diseases but some diseases do make their presence known and, particularly where there is shade, fusarium disease can cause disfigurement and bare places. By and large, it is more a disease of highly cultivated turf such as golf greens, but it is a thing to keep a look out for in autumn and in warm, humid conditions.

Regular Attention Required Although a great deal of work would seem necessary on a lawn to produce the best results, readers are reminded that in practice all that is required from the average householder is a few minutes per week *regularly*. If these are given conscientiously most of the troubles described in various parts of this book will not arise and, therefore, will not require the extra time to put them right.

Whether the lawn is 4 square yards or 4,000 square yards, whether it is regarded with awe or treated with no respect at all, whether it is regarded as a delicate plant to be crossed only on tip-toe, or is used as a play-ground by the family (and that of the neighbour), every patch of grass can be maintained in a suitable condition by intelligent effort.

The following chapters aim at the recognition of problems and give information on how to deal with them. Most troubles encountered on the domestic lawn are amenable to correction or, at least, very great improvement. Getting good results requires work, albeit pleasant, a measure of common sense and the timing of the operations in relation to weather and season.

CHAPTER NINE

MOWING

EVERY lawn—whether good or bad—must be kept mown
in order to survive as such, and in too many gardens this
is the only treatment the lawn ever gets. On the best-kept
lawns mowing takes up more time than any other operation, the grass being cut perhaps 50 or 60 times every
year. Therefore it is important to carry out mowing in
the right way, using the time involved to best advantage.

Effect of Mowing Any unshaded piece of ground given
regular mowing only will eventually produce a tolerable
sort of turf regardless of its state at first. In fact, mowing
has more influence on the quality of a lawn than any
other treatment, since it largely decides what plants can
survive. Most coarse and tufted grasses gradually disappear from the turf, and weeds which are common in
the flower bed such as groundsel, fat-hen, etc., will
quickly die out. The surviving residue consists of pros-
trate grasses such as bents and fescues, and coarser types
such as annual meadow grass and Yorkshire fog, together
with a number of weeds which are adapted to such conditions. These weeds include rosette types such as plantain, daisy and dandelion, as well as stragglers such as
clover and pearlwort.

Efficiency of Mowing Under ideal conditions the
mowing-machine should cut off all grass and other plants
in the turf which are longer than the cutting height to

47

which the mower has been adjusted. This aim will never be fully realized, but there are a number of ways in which the manner of mowing can be varied in order to improve its efficiency. In this way a finer and closer turf will be encouraged, and weeds which would otherwise grow undamaged by reason of their creeping stems will receive more punishment.

Frequency of Mowing All lawns should be mown often but not too keenly. Generally, the right frequency depends on the amount of growth which is taking place. In May and June mow twice or even three times a week, but ease off when growth slackens. This happens during summer drought or, in any case, in the early autumn. In a mild winter 'top' the lawn occasionally. This will keep in check the coarser grasses, such as perennial rye-grass, which have a longer growing season and would otherwise start the following year with an advantage over the dwarf grasses. Avoid mowing under very wet conditions, especially if there are many worm-casts; but do not delay more than a day or two.

Height of Cut A lawn should not be shaved down too closely. Cricket wickets may be cut as low as $\frac{1}{16}$ in., but such extreme punishment leaves behind many problems for the groundsman to solve which the lawn owner can well do without. A very close cut demands a perfectly smooth surface, otherwise the mower will scalp the turf. Weeds such as pearlwort and moss are also greatly encouraged by close cutting. For the ornamental lawn cutting at $\frac{1}{4}$ to $\frac{3}{8}$ in. will give best results, while for 'utility' lawns $\frac{1}{2}$ to 1 in. is sufficiently short. Experiments have

proved that lawn grasses cut at a lenient height three
times a week receive much less punishment than when
cut keenly only once a week.

Most mowers are provided with a scale indicating the
height of cut. These are not always accurate, especially
on an old machine. To check the height of cut on a roller
mower, the machine is turned over and a straight-edge
placed across the front and rear rollers. The height of cut
is measured from the straight-edge to the cutting edge
of the bottom fixed blade, and is conveniently measured

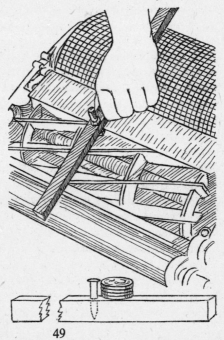

8. *The height of
the cutting blade
can be adjusted
by means of a
special gadget. It
can be measured
by penny thick-
nesses.*

49

by penny thicknesses (each approximately $\frac{1}{16}$ in.) A special gadget may be used instead of the straight-edge and pennies (see Fig. 8). It is important that this distance is identical on both sides of the machine, otherwise ridges will appear on the lawn after cutting. With a side-wheel machine the straight-edge is laid across the rear roller and the lowest point of each driving wheel in turn.

Boxing Cuttings Under normal conditions the grass-box should always be used. A firmer turf and less weed will result. It may be argued that the turf is being robbed of fertility in this way, but the fresh cuttings supply a feed that is well liked by earthworms and possibly contains viable seeds of weeds and unwanted grasses. It is far better to rot the clippings, and then to use them in a compost heap. They will then get back to the lawn in a properly decomposed state, mixed with soil, a season or two later. It is permissible to let the cuttings fly occasionally during a drought, so that they wither quickly, forming a mulch which will reduce evaporation of moisture from the surface.

Direction of Mowing Always push the mower continuously from one side of the lawn to the other, turn at the end, and return at the side of the strip just cut. Continuous running is less wearing on both operator and machine than 'push-pull' mowing and leaves a more uniform finish. Most of the pressure on the handles should be forward, leaving the machine to find its own level. Many mowers do, in fact, have a 'floating' handle that encourages this.

The direction of mowing should be changed each time

the lawn is cut. For example, a rectangular lawn should be mown up and down, then, on the next occasion, across, and then along the lines of each diagonal, each direction being taken in rotation. Much depends, however, on the size and shape of the individual lawn. A long, narrow lawn which can only be mown in one direction will often in time produce ridges across the line of mowing giving a 'wash-board' effect.

Brushing and Light Raking If any gardener should doubt the effect of raking the lawn let him mow once in the usual manner, rake the lawn thoroughly, then mow again and examine the clippings obtained. A neglected lawn will produce a mass of brown and dying stems as well as seed-heads of weeds and weed grasses. Once these are out of the way, the remaining turf will come through much stronger and cleaner. During the growing season the lawn should be scarified with a wire or Springbok rake every month or so, immediately before mowing, although avoiding drought periods. A whalebone brush or stiff yard broom can also be used as often as possible before mowing. It has a light scarifying effect, and will

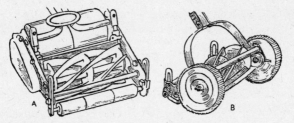

9. (*A*) *A roller mower.* (*B*) *A side-wheel mower.*

help to remove dew or other moisture from the grass before cutting.

Mower Rollers In damp conditions the front (if any) and rear rollers of the mower should be kept clean of worm-casts and accumulation of clippings; otherwise the machine cannot work at the setting to which it has been adjusted.

Types of Mowers A sharp mower is essential. When buying a mower there are many points to look for, the most important of which is the number of cuts which are made per yard run of the machine. This depends on the speed of the cutting cylinder, obtained by gearing or chain drive from the main roller or driving wheels, and also on the number of blades attached to the cylinder. The mower should also be close coupled, that is, with a short distance between the front roller and the cutting cylinder, so that skinning of the surface does not occur when minor bumps on the lawn are passed over. A roller-driven mower (Fig. 9, A), though costlier, will give more satisfactory service than the side-wheel type (Fig. 9, B). It gives better that striped effect (Fig. 10) which looks so well on a new-mown lawn; the higher gearing gives more cuts per yard run. Mowing right up to the edge is simplified, as the roller mower can be pushed along overhanging the edge without much risk of scalping the surface. On the other hand, a side-wheel machine is more efficient for use after the lawn has been scarified, since there is no front roller which will press down the stems of coarse grasses and weeds which have been raised by the rake.

Most practical greenkeepers seem to agree that hand

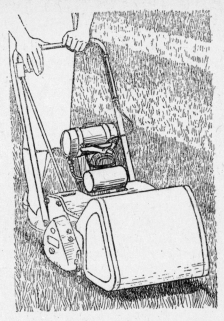

10. *A motor-mower in use. Note the striped effect of the finished work.*

mowing gives the best finish, but for the gardener with a large lawn some form of power may be necessary to save time and energy. A heavy motor mower gives unwanted compaction and skinning at the turns. Some manufacturers, however, have considerably reduced the weight of their machines, and have thus largely eliminated these faults (Fig. 10).

A compromise between hand and motor is the mower having only the cutting cylinder power driven, and although the machine is still pushed by hand, most of the donkey work is eliminated. Some of the smaller power mowers are driven by an electric motor, and these give quiet and efficient service on many lawns. The trailing cable is seldom a disadvantage if systematically handled. **Adjustment and Maintenance** As with any other mechanical equipment, the mower should be kept oiled and greased, and clean when not in use. This applies particularly in the autumn, when the mower may not be in use again for some months.

Apart from routine cleaning, at some time during each winter the mower deserves a thorough cleaning, sharpening and overhauling. With the more expensive and powered models, it is preferable to have this done by the makers.

CHAPTER TEN

FERTILIZER TREATMENT AND THE USE OF LIME

GRASS needs a large number of mineral elements from the soil, but only three commonly require attention from the plant nutrient point of view. They are nitrogen, phosphorus and potassium, and of these without question nitrogen is the most important.

Nitrogenous Fertilizers   The most important organic fertilizers supplying nitrogen are dried blood and hoof and horn meal. They have their uses for lawns, but must be used with great discretion, since they tend to encourage a soft, weedy and worm-infested turf. Inorganic fertilizers which supply nitrogen are sulphate of ammonia, nitrate of soda and Nitrochalk. All these are quick acting and all can be used in appropriate circumstances, but undoubtedly the nitrogen fertilizer which suits most circumstances is sulphate of ammonia, and the correct rate is $\frac{1}{2}$ oz. per square yard.

Phosphatic Fertilizers   Superphosphate, bonemeal and steamed bone flour are the most common fertilizers of this type for turf, and of these the best is superphosphate used at, say, 1 oz. per square yard.

Potassic Fertilizers   Sulphate of potash, muriate of potash or potash salts may be used to supply potassium where needed. This plant food is not so frequently in short supply as the other two, but is said to have some

benefits in drought and disease resistance. For this reason
a little is commonly put into mixtures for turf, and sulphate of potash ($\frac{1}{4}$ oz. per square yard) is the most suitable
for this purpose.

Compound Fertilizers A compound fertilizer is one
supplying more than one of the three chief plant foods.
It may be a mixture of several fertilizers, but ammonium
phosphate and potassium nitrate are examples of concentrated compound fertilizers. Neither of these is very
common, and both are usually rather expensive.

Complete Fertilizers For lawn or garden a complete
fertilizer is one which supplies all three of the main plant
foods—nitrogen, phosphorus (phosphate) and potassium
(potash). A complete fertilizer is a compound fertilizer,
and for lawns the backbone of the mixture should consist of: sulphate of ammonia, superphosphate, sulphate
of potash (see page 55).

Soot Soot is a very variable product containing 2% to
11% of nitrogen. It may be used on the lawn, but is
probably put to better advantage if applied to the cultivated parts of the garden.

By-products Used as Fertilizers Many by-product
materials are considered very useful fertilizers. They
range from castor meal to cocoa waste, and from Peruvian
or fish guano to poultry manure. Excellent in the right
place, these should not normally be used on the lawn.

Sulphate of Iron Although necessary to correct soil defi-
ciencies in some parts of the world, in lawn management
sulphate of iron is used, not as a fertilizer but as a turf
conditioner. For this purpose it is applied in the calcined

form at the rate of about $\frac{1}{6}$ oz. per square yard, usually in admixture with fertilizer. Used thus, it improves the colour of the lawn, helps to keep out weeds, worms and diseases, and encourages the finer lawn grasses. It is also used as a weed-killer (see *Lawn Sands*, Chapter Eleven) and as a fungicide (Chapter Twelve).

A Year's Treatment for the Lawn Many lawns have been maintained in excellent condition for years without any fertilizer treatment at all. Undoubtedly, however, there are countless lawns which would benefit from a little feed. Often this can be met by the application of a dressing of sulphate of ammonia at $\frac{1}{2}$ oz. per square yard bulked up with 4 oz. of carrier at an opportune moment in the growing season, usually in the spring. Two or three dressings may be given between the months of April and August (inclusive), but one may well be sufficient. As an alternative to several dressings of sulphate of ammonia, one or more dressings of equal parts sulphate of ammonia and hoof and horn meal at $\frac{1}{2}$ oz. per square yard (plus carrier) may be used. The hoof and horn is slower acting than the sulphate of ammonia, so that the effect of using the mixture is to spread the growth stimulation over a longer period.

Where the soil is low in other mineral plant foods a complete fertilizer is required. A suitable mixture for the lawn (rates per square yard) is:

Mixture A: $\frac{1}{2}$ oz. of sulphate of ammonia

  1 to 2 oz. of superphosphate

  $\frac{1}{4}$ oz. of sulphate of potash

This simple mixture is excellent for the lawn, but is

inferior in keeping quality in that it goes hard and lumpy. If mixed up immediately with not less than four to eight times its weight of carrier, such as dry screened soil or sand, and then applied to the turf, this difficulty does not arise.

A useful modification of the above mixture with improved keeping quality and possessing ingredients with varying speeds of action is (rates per square yard):

Mixture B: ½ oz. of sulphate of ammonia
   ¼ oz. of hoof and horn meal (or dried blood)
   1 oz. of superphosphate
   ¼ oz. of steamed bone flour or bonemeal
   ¼ oz. of sulphate of potash

The best time to apply these mixtures is the spring, and with advantage in most cases ⅙ oz. calcined sulphate of iron per square yard may be added. If insufficient improvement is effected, then later in the season further treatment with sulphate of ammonia may be given.

Application of Fertilizers For successful results fertilizers must be distributed uniformly over the surface of the lawn. The first step is to mix up the fertilizer with a considerable quantity of sand or screened, dry soil of not less than four to eight times the weight of the fertilizer. The purpose of this bulking agent is to minimize direct scorch and to make even application easier. The bulked-up mixture may be spread by hand (Fig. 11) (not shovel) or good fertilizer distributor. Hand application is quite satisfactory provided that great care is taken. When treating the vegetable garden, fertilizers may be mixed into the

11. *Applying fertilizer or top-dressing.*

soil with a rake, but this is not so on the lawn and so distribution should aim at giving every square inch its proper share. As with sowing grass seed, it is of help to divide up the fertilizer into two parts and sow in transverse directions; in fact, with large lawns it is worth while dividing up the lawn into sections and weighing out the portion for each separate section into two lots. Watering-in should not be carried out unless application is followed by prolonged dry weather.

Some lawn owners are interested in applying lawn feeds in solution. With suitable fertilizers this method may be used, but it is not recommended because of the tendency of solution to soak preferentially into hollows and soft places, thus giving uneven distribution.

Lime As in the garden, when the soil becomes too acid it is necessary to apply lime to correct the over-acidity. Over-acidity in lawns is comparatively rare, however, and the best lawn grasses thrive under slightly acid conditions. Lime encourages earthworms and weeds in turf, and, therefore, it should not be used unless a considerable degree of acidity is known to be present. On the comparatively rare occasions when lime is necessary, the correct form to use is carbonate of lime (ground limestone or ground chalk). Lime should be applied in the autumn or winter months at a rate appropriate to the nature of the soil and its degree of acidity, and this will usually be 2 to 4 oz. per square yard.

CHAPTER ELEVEN

WEEDS AND WEED-KILLING

GARDENERS are usually more concerned with the removal of weeds from their lawns than with the identification of the weeds or the reasons for them. A truism it may be, but, as always, prevention is better than cure, and some understanding of weeds and their causes helps us to prevent and eliminate them.

Weeds are plants which are present though not wanted in a particular situation. This means for our purpose all plants except good turf-forming species, and includes coarse, unsightly or unsuitable grasses.

The best and cheapest approach to a weed-free lawn is that of management. A thick and healthy sward resulting from correct fertilizer treatment and good, regular mowing resists invasion and spread of weeds. When an odd small weed does appear in an otherwise clean lawn, the wise will attend to it immediately so that it does not grow into a problem! Hand weeding is not to be despised as a method of attack, especially where weeds are comparatively few.

Coarse Grasses Common examples of these are couch grass (*Agropyron repens*), Yorkshire fog (*Holcus lanatus*) and creeping soft grass (*Holcus mollis*). Perennial ryegrass (*Lolium perenne*), a useful constituent of some lawns, must be regarded as a weed in the finest fescue and bent lawns. Annual meadow-grass (*Poa annua*) is another grass of doubtful value.

Weed grasses such as rye-grass or annual meadow-grass may be in the seed-bed, they may be introduced with the rest of the grass seed or they may invade an established lawn. Once they appear in a lawn they are likely to spread, and should be dealt with at the earliest opportunity. There are no chemical treatments suitable for eliminating one kind of grass from among other grasses, and so the unwanted plants must be dealt with by hand weeding. Surface scarification in conjunction with mowing is useful against Yorkshire fog and creeping soft grass. This may be effected with a wire rake or even with an ordinary garden rake. More drastic but very useful is the method of making a series of 'criss-cross' vertical slits in individual patches with a sharp knife. Under such treatment the invader is gradually replaced by the desirable grasses. Annual meadow grass is a prolific seeder and spreads rapidly in a lawn, especially when management is at fault. Some measure of control can be obtained by brushing up the seed-heads and mowing keenly to remove them.

Annual and Biennial Weeds   Annual weeds are usually eliminated by constant mowing, and few biennials survive this constant defoliation. Shepherd's-purse (*Capsella bursa-pastoris*), which behaves as an annual or biennial (possibly even perennial), is sometimes a nuisance, and it can be removed with the selective hormone weed-killers discussed later. Wild carrot (*Daucus carota*) and spear thistle (*Cirsium vulgare*) are biennials which sometimes occur and these also can be treated with selective weed-killers.

Perennial Weeds Most lawn weeds are perennials, the worst offenders being:

Creeping buttercup (*Ranunculus repens* L.)
Ribwort plantain (*Plantago lanceolata* L.)
Broad-leaved plantain (*Plantago major* L.)
Daisy (*Bellis perennis* L.)
Dandelion (*Taraxacum officinale* Web.)
Mouse-ear chickweed (*Cerastium vulgatum* L.)
Wild white clover (*Trifolium repens* L.)
Yarrow (*Achillea millefolium* L.)
Pearlwort (*Sagina procumbens* L.)

WEED-KILLERS

There are numerous materials available today for controlling weeds, ranging from those of the lawn-sand type, which are by no means out-dated, to the more modern selective weed-killers. The problem, of course, is to remove weeds without harming the grass or at least to do as little harm to the grass as possible.

Lawn Sands Lawn sands are weed-killers (not merely sands to put on lawns!), and they can either be used for spot-treating individual weeds where weeds are not widespread or they can be applied to the whole lawn. A good mixture for general use is: 3 parts of sulphate of ammonia, 1 part of calcined sulphate of iron, 20 parts of sharp sand. This should be applied at 4 oz. per square yard, preferably on a dewy morning during a fine spell of weather. Great care should be taken to ensure that even distribution is obtained, otherwise there is danger that excessive scorching of the grass may follow. It must be realized that lawn sands depend for their action on burning out the weeds. They are very successful against pearlwort and daisies. More concentrated mixtures than the above, e.g. with less sand, may be used for spot-treatment only.

Selective Weed-killers Since 1945 new weed-killers have appeared which are more selective in nature; that is, they are designed to kill the weeds while harming the grass little if at all. In practice they do retard the growth of the grass slightly for a short time.

Selective weed-killers will control most weeds, but their degree of control is variable, and in general, while broad-leaved weeds such as plantains are easily controlled, weeds such as yarrow and pearlwort are more resistant and repeat applications are necessary to effect a satis-factory control.

Selective weed-killers are based on chemicals known as plant growth regulators or plant hormones, of which the two most important are MCPA and 2 : 4 D. These are sold as proprietary weed-killers containing one or other of these chemicals as their active ingredient, and may be obtained from most horticultural sundriesmen. More recently other products have appeared containing 2 : 4 : 5 T or mixtures of 2 : 4 D and 2 : 4 : 5 T. These are designed primarily for brushwood control, and are per-haps slightly more effective against the more resistant weeds; but great care is needed in their use as they scorch the grass.

How to Apply Selective weed-killers can be applied in

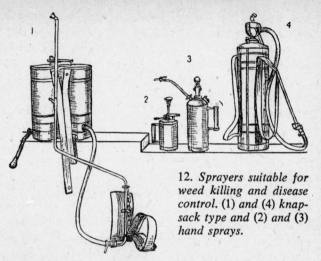

12. *Sprayers suitable for weed killing and disease control. (1) and (4) knapsack type and (2) and (3) hand sprays.*

either liquid or powder form, and it is generally found that the liquid form gives the best control. For the application of the liquid weed-killer it is best to dilute with water and apply as a fine spray using a small hand sprayer or a knapsack sprayer, of which there are a variety on the market (Fig. 12). A watering-can with a fine rose may also be used, and it has advantages, since the larger drops produced are less likely to drift on to flower-beds.

Powder weed-killer can be applied by hand or by a fertilizer distributor, but special care should be exercised to obtain an even distribution.

Great care is needed in the application of these hormone weed-killers in order to ensure uniform coverage and to prevent damage to the grass. During the application the lawn should be marked out in strips, and each strip treated in turn, great care being taken not to overlap.

Instructions regarding the rate of application should be carefully observed otherwise there is a danger of serious damage to the grass, since these materials are selective only at the correct rate of application. No trace of weed-killer should reach plants in beds surrounding the lawn, since they are likely to be damaged or even killed. If contamination is suspected, copious watering of affected plants may reduce the ill-effects.

When to Apply The time of application should be carefully chosen. The best conditions are during fine warm weather when the soil is moist and both grass and weeds are growing vigorously. For best results, no rain should fall for at least twenty-four hours after the weed-killer has been applied, while calm conditions minimize the risk of contaminating flower-beds. Treatment can fit into normal mowing routine provided that no mowing is done for one or two days after treatment. Good results may be obtained at any time of the year when there is growth, but late spring and early summer are the best times. It is usually advantageous to apply a light dressing of fertilizer (e.g. $\frac{1}{2}$ oz. of sulphate of ammonia and 4 oz. of sand per square yard) a week or so before weed-killing to ensure active growth of both grass and weeds. Given good conditions, one application of weed-killer may give satisfactory results, but one or two repeat applications at about monthly intervals may be necessary for resistant weeds.

Individual Weeds Selective weed-killers may be used for spot-treatment of individual weeds, but it is usually best to apply them over the whole area. For most weeds there is little to choose between the two main types of selective weed-killers (MCPA and 2 : 4 D), but for pearlwort the former is preferred.

Effect The first effects of selective weed-killers can be seen in twisting and freak growth of the weeds. This is noticeable within a day or two after application of the weed-killer, but the weeds may not finally disappear for several weeks.

MOSS

Moss has a great capacity for spreading rapidly through a lawn due to the fact that in addition to vegetative means of propagation it is able to reproduce by spores which are formed in very great numbers in small capsules. No one factor can be stated to be solely responsible for the presence of moss, but infertility, over acidity, very wet conditions and also mowing too closely all may contribute. Anything which leads to bare and thin places gives moss an easy means of access to the lawn. Of a variety of mosses to be found in lawns two common ones are *Ceratodon purpureus* and *Hypnum cupressiforme*. The best means of control is to discover the reasons for its presence and try to change these conditions. This can best be done by maintaining a good, dense sward, but once moss has become established corrective treatments have to be adopted. During the growing season mixtures of the lawn-sand type are useful for this purpose, a good mixture being: $\frac{1}{4}$ oz. of sulphate of ammonia, $\frac{1}{4}$ oz. of calcined sulphate of iron, 4 oz. of sand per square yard.

Such a mixture blackens the moss, after which it should be raked out. When it is not desirable to stimulate the grass, the sulphate of ammonia may be omitted and the sulphate of iron and sand only used. Alternatively $\frac{1}{4}$ to $\frac{1}{2}$ oz. of sulphate of iron may be watered on in $\frac{1}{2}$ to 1 gallon of water per square yard. All these treatments are best applied in dry weather, and may be repeated two or three times as required. If the moss occupies considerable patches ugly scars may be left, and these should be raked and sown with seed.

ALGAE AND LICHENS

There are a considerable number of terrestrial algae, but very few are known to appear on lawns. The only one which is liable to be encountered is *Nostoc*, which occurs as small blue-green gelatinous clumps. It is encouraged by a wet, greasy surface, due to excessive compaction of the surface layers of soil. Control can be obtained by using either sulphate of copper applied at the rate of 1 oz. in 25 gallons of water per 100 square yards, or sulphate of iron applied at the rate of 1 oz. in 2 gallons of water per 4 square yards.

Occasionally lichens are found growing in turf. These are often indicative of over acidity, and are sometimes found generally when, due to poor soil conditions, the grass is not growing well and the sward is rather thin.

Lichens are composite organisms, being part alga and part fungus. The commonest lichen encountered in lawns is *Peltigera canina*, a species producing leafy lobes which smother the grass. As lichens are usually characteristic of poor soils, control is achieved by first treating the turf with sulphate of iron at $\frac{1}{4}$ oz. per square yard bulked with 4 oz. of sharp sand, and then encouraging a stronger growth of grass by suitable fertilizer treatment.

CHAPTER TWELVE

PESTS AND DISEASES OF THE LAWN

PESTS

Earthworms In the garden earthworms are desirable inhabitants of the soil, stirring, mixing and aerating it. They will do this in a lawn also, but here their disadvantages outweigh any advantages. The casts they produce make the turf muddy and uneven. When flattened by feet or machines these impede drainage and provide points for invasion by undesirable species of grasses and weeds. Worms are one of the commonest causes of lawn deterioration; their eradication assists in the production of a dense, clean sward.

Earthworms may be eradicated by applying either a liquid which penetrates the soil and expels them, or by putting on materials which are poisonous to them and which will kill them in the soil. Some expellent types of worm-killer also kill the worms.

Expellent worm-killers should be used during warm or mild weather when the worms are working near the surface. The safest kinds are mowrah meal, derris and potassium permanganate. Mowrah meal purchased as 'finely ground' should be applied at 6 to 8 oz. to the square yard, and watered into the soil with at least 1 gallon of water to the square yard. Froth will appear, and shortly afterwards worms will come to the surface, where they die. They should be gathered up. A repeat application will be necessary in two years or perhaps less. Derris powder, containing 1% rotenone, applied at 1 oz. per square yard watered in, is also effective. If it contains 2% rotenone, the amount used per square yard should be halved. As mowrah and derris contain fish poisons, they should not be used where there is a risk of drainage into fish-ponds. Potassium permanganate at ½ oz. dissolved in 1 gallon water to 1 square yard is effective, simple and safe. In price mowrah and potassium permanganate are comparable, while derris is more expensive.

Lead arsenate is a worm-killer of the non-expellent type. It is applied dry, again preferably when the worms are active, at 2 oz. per square yard. Immediate results should not be expected, but control will last for several years. Animals should be kept off the turf until the powder has washed in.

Mowing, fertilization and top-dressing have an effect on the reinvasion of turf with earthworms and on their activity. Leaving the grass long, mowing without the box on and heavy applications of organic manures favour earthworm activity. Worms are encouraged by liming or the application of shell containing sand, but, on the other hand, materials such as peat have the opposite effect. Sulphate of ammonia and sulphate of iron dressings discourage them. Reinvasion of worm-free turf generally takes place from surrounding wormy areas and often from borders.

Leather-jackets These are the grub of the crane-fly or daddy-longlegs (Fig. 13). While most turf will stand a

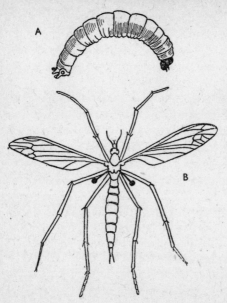

13. *Crane-fly or daddy-longlegs (B). The larva (A) is a leather-jacket, and can do extensive damage.*

few leather-jackets, they can cause extensive damage to it (as well as to other plants and crops) when they are present in large numbers. Mild, wet weather in late August and September favours them. The grubs, which in September may be up to $\frac{1}{4}$ in. long, are susceptible to drought, so a dry September results in big mortality. They do most damage in early spring, while birds preying on them cause turf damage in their search. The grubs can be killed by dusting the turf with either $\frac{1}{2}$ oz. of 5% DDT powder or 1 oz. $3\frac{1}{2}$% BHC powder per square yard. Lead arsenate at $\frac{1}{2}$ oz. per square yard will also control them. The insecticide should be put on in the autumn of the year if leather-jackets are noted.

Ants Ants are sometimes troublesome in lawns. They may be controlled by dusting the affected turf with 1 oz. of 5% BHC dust to the square yard.

Other Pests Cockchafer grubs, dung-beetle grubs, cut-worms and fever flies may do a little damage to turf, but probably more damage is done by birds searching for them. DDT or BHC dusts or lead arsenate may be used for their control.

DISEASES

Fusarium Patch Disease This is by far the commonest fungal disease of turf in this country. In autumn particularly, but also during muggy periods at other times of the year, small patches of yellowish, dying grass may appear on the turf. Under damp, humid conditions these patches will increase in size if unchecked, and adjacent patches may join up (Fig. 14). Fungal threads may be seen round the edges of the patches, and they and the spores of the fungus, produced on the patches, are the means by which the disease develops and is spread.

To prevent the disease, the turf should be kept vigorous by cultural and fertilizer treatments; yet it should not be in any way forced. Slight under-feeding the turf rather than over-feeding should be the motto, and the use of nitrogenous fertilizers should be avoided after mid-August. Try to keep the grass plants as dry as possible by switching off dew and opening up hedges and other screens if they prevent air movement over the turf.

14. *Fusarium patch disease is a disfiguring fungal disease of turf.*

Annual meadow-grass is most susceptible to the disease, and should be kept out if at all practicable. Other species and strains of turf grasses vary in resistance to the disease.

Because it is easier to prevent than to cure, some lawn owners use fungicides to protect the turf from attack by the fungus before any signs of the disease appear, but the protective covering of fungicide on the grass plants should be renewed every seven days or so during the danger period. Fungicides may be used to cure the disease, after appearance of course, and in some cases the curative rate of application is higher than the protective rate. There are several reliable proprietary turf fungicides available. One contains the dye malachite green, others are mixtures of calomel and corrosive sublimate while yet another contains an organo-mercury compound. These are effective against the disease when properly applied according to the maker's directions. It should be noted that mercury compounds are poisonous. Wet fungicides should be put on with a suitable sprayer (Fig. 12); dry ones should be dusted on evenly, and the whole turf area should be treated. It may be necessary to repeat the application perhaps several times to cure the disease. A good emergency treatment for the amateur is to apply with a watering-can a solution of $\frac{1}{4}$ oz. sulphate of iron in $\frac{1}{2}$ gallon of water to 1 square yard. This may cure a mild attack or stem a severe one sufficiently or at any rate until a more recognized turf fungicide can be applied.

Corticium Disease This is a disfiguring disease of turf which generally appears about mid-summer, but it rarely does a great deal of damage. It is commonly found on turf that has been starved. Young patches of the disease are roughly circular, but become less regular in outline later. Attacked grass has a bleached look, and small, pink, branched needles of the fungus develop on many of the blades and sheaths. These fungal needles can live at least two years after falling to the ground, and can be the source of another season's patches. Fescues are most severely attacked, but other species may suffer as well. To control the disease the vigour of the sward should be increased by cultural methods and by feeding it. A fungicide containing malachite green is particularly effective in controlling this disease.

Fairy Rings There are many cap fungi which grow in rings in turf. Their growth in the soil may be associated with rings of dark green grass, or in some cases two green rings with a bare zone between may be noted. Fairy rings can be disfiguring, particularly the latter type which in this country are most commonly caused by *Marasmius oreades*. If the soil in one of these latter rings is inspected, a characteristic strong mushroom smell will be noted, and the soil will be seen to be filled with fungal threads to a considerable extent. To get rid of this type of ring, the fungus-infected soil should be removed completely and cleanly. A safe margin round this soil should also be removed, and all of it tipped where it cannot start new rings. Water the sides and bottom of the excavation, avoiding surrounding grass, with a solution of 1 part of 40% formaldehyde solution to 159 parts of water to wet them well. Cover the excavation with sacks, and after a week fill in with clean soil. After a further 14 days, firm-up and sow or turf it.

Puff-ball and mushroom rings show a green single ring or ribbon of grass with the fruiting bodies of the fungus growing through. Control of these rings is sometimes effected by brushing a calomel-corrosive sublimate fungicide down fork holes in them, or applying a solution of 1 oz. of malchite green, with a good wetting agent, in 28 gallons of water and applying it at 1 gallon to the square yard to the pricked ring. Repeat applications are necessary.

Dollar Spot   This disease is difficult to recognize without expert assistance. Mercurial turf fungicides should be tried.

Damping-off   These diseases have been dealt with in Chapter Seven.

CHAPTER THIRTEEN

SURFACE MAINTENANCE OPERATIONS

To many people all that is required to maintain a good lawn is a good heavy roller, but unfortunately this is by no means the complete answer it is supposed to be. A true surface is best obtained by means of regular top-dressing, provided the irregularities are not too marked, and then a more radical approach is necessary.

Correcting Minor Irregularities Minor surface irregularities can be gradually smoothed out by *regular* applications of 2 to 7 lb. per square yard of bulky materials, such as soily compost or good top-spit soil and similar materials, which are known as top-dressings. Such top-dressings should not be applied too thickly, say over ¼ in.

15. *Top-dressing should be rubbed into the turf.*

16. *How to use a hollow-tine fork.*

in thickness, or the grass may be smothered. The dressing should be fairly dry so that after spreading it can be well worked into the turf by means of a straight-edge such as the back of a rake, or a drag-brush or drag-mat, or even by hand (Fig. 15). Localized small rises may be eased by taking out cores with a hollow-tine fork if one is available (Fig. 16).

Top-dressing The use of bulky materials for top-dressing need not be confined to lawns with a markedly uneven surface. Top-dressing can be used to improve the surface gradually by building up on top a better layer with

78

improved moisture characteristics. Compost is the ideal top-dressing, and in turf management compost means light loam soil which has been enriched in organic matter in a suitable compost heap. It is different from much of the compost used in the garden, which tends to be regarded as a substitute for farmyard manure. A compost heap for turf is constructed by laying down alternate layers of 4 to 6 in. of well-rotted organic material such as farmyard manure and 6 to 9 in. of loam top-spit soil. Some waste organic material may have to undergo a prior rotting down. The compost heap should stand at least 12 months, and may require turning during this period. When required for use, the heap is broken down in vertical slices with a spade and the compost riddled before use. At this stage, adjustments may still be made before application by mixing in sand or other materials as required.

Many materials other than compost may be used as top-dressings under appropriate conditions. These include loam soil, sharp sand, coke breeze, charcoal, leaf-mould, dried sewage, peat and, of course, mixtures of these to give a substitute compost. Sand for use as a top-dressing should be sharp, gritty and free from lime in the form of shell. It must be differentiated from 'lawn sand', which is a weed-killer.

The texture of the material applied should be light and porous, but possessing sufficient organic matter to help moisture retention. If the original soil of the lawn is very heavy the top-dressing should be very light and sandy, while if the original soil is very sandy the top-dressing should be rich in organic matter. Some ingenuity can be exercised in the production of a suitable mixture, and the following example should indicate the lines to work on:

6 parts of screened loam soil, 3 parts of sharp washed river sand, 1 part of fine peat or leaf-mould.

For bowling-greens and the like top-dressing material is sometimes subjected to partial sterilization, chiefly to eliminate weed seeds. Few amateurs will go to this trouble, but no doubt they will take steps to avoid introducing weeds into the lawn with the compost.

Correcting Major Irregularities   It is almost impossible to get rid of severe irregularities of surface by top-dressing alone, and it becomes necessary to give special attention to individual holes or mounds as the case may be.

Mounds and hollows should be dealt with by stripping off the turf and removing or adding as much earth as required. Sometimes work can be saved by rolling back the turf in coils like a Swiss-roll after first making cuts with an edging-iron at 12-in. spacings. Care must be taken that at the end there is sufficient top-soil for the turf to grow, and in extreme cases top-soil may have to be removed as well as turf so that adjustments in levels may be affected in the subsoil. The replaced turf should be top-dressed to fill in the cracks and to encourage the turf to knit together.

There is a less drastic method of dealing with hollows, which does not involve the removal of the turf but does require two operators. The procedure is as follows:

First make an initial cut of the required length with a

flat spade, along one edge of the area which is to be lifted. A second cut is then made parallel to the first and 9 to 12 in. away from it. Next make a third cut, so that there are now two 'loose' strips of turf, the cuts having been made 6 to 9 in. deep. Now raise the first strip by inserting a fork through strip two into strip one and levering with the handle. More than one fork may be required if a fairly big hollow is being dealt with. While the turf is held up, the second operator should stuff sufficient top-soil under the turf as evenly as possible, whereupon the turf is allowed to go back and is trodden down firmly and the whole job finished off by rubbing in top-dressing.

Rolling   Rolling can be very useful for smoothing the surface and firming up the turf. Indeed, a good roll each spring is a decided advantage in eliminating the excessive softness which usually results from the winter weather. Unfortunately rolling is often overdone. While it will smooth out the surface it does so only at a price: that of excess consolidation of the bumps resulting in inferior turf on these areas because of the restrictions imposed on water movement and root development. Smoothing out the surface is best effected by suitable top-dressings.

Aeration   There are two kinds of aeration—that which affects mainly the surface and that which attempts to be more fundamental and influence the top-soil. Surface aeration is brought about by scarifying the surface with a wire rake, or with an ordinary garden rake if great care is taken. Such treatment can be carried out with advantage on most lawns throughout the year. Normally only light treatment is wanted, but at the end of the summer and again in the early spring more thorough treatment helps to remove moss and dead fibre and to encourage the grass to tiller. Scarification as required during the growing season prevents the accumulation of excess fibre, and in conjunction with mowing helps to eliminate weeds such as yarrow and clover.

The more fundamental type of aeration aims at helping air and moisture penetration into the surface soil when this has become impeded through over-rolling or merely through repeated mowing and treading in normal use. Some types of soil are inclined to pack down more tightly than others, of course, and on a sandy, open soil this kind of aeration will rarely be necessary.

Aeration operations for the top-soil involve the use of some kind of fork. An ordinary garden fork may be used to ease up the turf, but unfortunately the process, while successful in removing consolidation, is likely to lead to a most uneven surface!

It is much better, therefore, to obtain a special fork for the purpose, a fork with prongs or tines designed to go straight in and out without disturbing the turf. Such a fork can be purchased with either solid tines or hollow tines or with interchangeable tines. Each type of tine has its uses in particular circumstances. Where forking is carried out regularly or in less severe circumstances solid tines are best, but for relieving excessive compression hollow tines are far superior. Hollow-tine forks take cores out of the turf and deposit them on the surface (Fig. 16). The result is that the surrounding earth can expand into the holes, thus relieving compression and allowing porosity to develop so that air and moisture can get into the soil freely. The cores deposited on the surface may be allowed to dry out and then broken up to form a top-dressing, or they may be swept off and placed on the compost heap. Normally the holes may be left open but, if desired, the opportunity may be taken to work in materials such as sharp sand to improve the porosity of the soil permanently.

CHAPTER FOURTEEN

DRAINAGE AND WATERING

Drainage Even the most ardent lawn lover is likely to feel that it is asking too much to expect him to start draining operations! Yet it is not the lot of every gardener to have his lawn in a free-draining situation, such as on a sandy loam soil over a porous sub-soil. There are two facets of this drainage problem on lawns. They are firstly, getting excess water through the surface, and secondly getting rid of this water afterwards.

Surface Drainage Getting the water away from the surface is the first problem, and porous, freely permeable top-soil is required. Over-consolidation such as is caused by unwise rolling, especially if earthworms are present, is the one thing to avoid. Spiking and forking operations improve the surface permeability, and should be undertaken when required. It is very fortunate that grass, itself, growing in a vigorous turf with a well-developed root system, is one of the best improvers of soil structure and porosity so that water and air penetration of the surface is only impeded as a result of ill-treatment, e.g. on over-played football fields.

Land Drainage When excess rainfall penetrates the surface soil it ultimately reaches the water-table, and it is important that this should not come too near the surface and the grass roots. If it does so for prolonged periods, then stagnation results, the soil becomes foul smelling, the vigour of the sward is impaired and it is muddy and wears badly, while weeds such as moss and toad-rush may invade the lawn.

Draining a lawn is a comparatively simple operation provided there is somewhere for the water to go, and this often causes a difficulty which can only be surmounted by the construction of a soak-pit filled with rubble which will take the collected water away from the drainage system quite quickly and allow it to seep away slowly afterwards.

For the average lawn a very simple drainage system is adequate. Very often a single drain line running across the site and emptying into the sump or other disposal point will suffice. The drain may take the form of 3-in. clayware agricultural tiles (pipes) laid at a depth of 1 ft. 6 in. to 3 ft. and covered with clinker and ash to

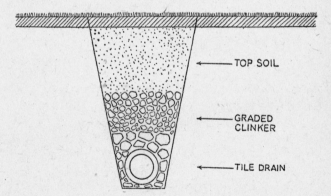

17. *The pipes are laid on the bottom of the trench and covered with clinker and ash.*

within 6 in. of the surface before the final covering of top-soil (Fig. 17). Alternatively, instead of the tiles the bottom of the trench may be filled loosely with stones which allow water movement, and these covered with clinker, ash and top-soil as before. It is important that the drain should have an even fall towards the outlet.

On very large lawns more complex drainage systems may be required, and these should be constructed on the recognized principles of field drainage, always having regard to the better standard required for lawns.

Drought Resistance and Watering Turf with a deep, well-developed root system is more drought resistant than shallow rooted turf, and all efforts should be made to attain good roots. A good drainage system, surprisingly enough, improves drought resistance by encouraging a good deep root system.

The nature of the soil itself has a considerable influence on the moisture-holding capacity, and hence on the vigour of the turf in dry weather. When constructing a new lawn it is useful to incorporate organic materials such as peat into the soil, particularly when this is light in texture. On an established lawn peat and other suitable organic material should be used in top-dressings for the same reasons.

The kinds of grass in the lawn also affect the resistance to drought. Outstanding for resistance are the fine-leaved fescues while annual meadow-grass is often the first to be affected.

Watering Watering, of course, is a mixed blessing. It does keep the lawn green and flourishing in dry weather, but on the other hand it encourages certain types of weed and keeps alive inferior grasses, such as annual meadow-grass, which, on the best lawns at any rate, could be allowed to die out with advantage.

When water is to be used, the rules are simple: Water early (before the grass starts to wilt), water copiously and water often. In other words, once watering is decided upon the job should be done thoroughly. A great many minor rules of watering are sometimes voiced, but these are very subsidiary to those already stated. It is, however, an advantage to use air-warm soft water when possible,

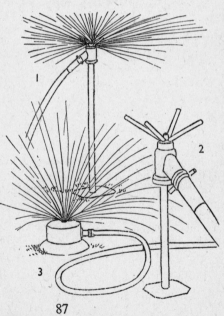

18. (1) and (2) are the same rotary sprinkler, in action in (1). A simple type of sprinkler is (3).

and to apply in the evening rather than in direct sunlight. The water need not be pure as for drinking purposes, but should be free from harmful contamination which sometimes reaches streams and rivers from industry.

Water should be applied by some simple type of sprinkler such as those shown in Fig. 18. A fine spray and even distribution are wanted, and neither is likely to be attained by the direct use of a hose-pipe. The householder will usually find that the mains are his only supply of water. The water is quite suitable, of course, but unfortunately its use for lawns and gardens is likely to be prohibited just when it is most required.

CHAPTER FIFTEEN

BANKS, VERGES, TURF UNDER TREES AND TENNIS COURTS

Banks The treatment of banks should be similar to other lawn areas. Their construction has already been discussed in Chapter One and the necessity for gentle slopes indicated. There is always a tendency, however, for them to become starved and to dry out during the summer, thus letting weeds and moss get a hold. Fertilizer treatment is therefore necessary. Furthermore, to enable water (rain or artificial) to penetrate to the roots rather than to run off, forking should be carried out from time to time. Given some reasonable amount of maintenance, moss and weed invasion can be checked, and a well-grassed bank certainly looks very attractive.

The grading of the bank should be such that the upper edge is gently rounded; if it is not, corrections should be made, since skinning with the mower will inevitably occur. Likewise, at the foot there should be a gradual tapering out to the level below so that the mower can get in to make a uniform cut.

It is often advisable to put in a catch-drain at the foot of a bank, this being all the more necessary if a tennis court is sited on this level.

Verges A well-maintained verge is undoubtedly an attraction in a garden. If irregular, too narrow, scalped or weedy, it is better discarded or renewed. Treatment should be on the same lines as for the rest of the grass areas, but pay particular attention to the trimming of the edges. Neatness is all important. The half-moon edging-iron must only be used to an absolute minimum, since obviously on each occasion the width of the verge is decreased. The use of hand clippers (or long-handled shears) should be regular to obtain the desired neatly trimmed appearance. A roller, not a side-wheel, mower should preferably be used for cutting.

Besides being more pleasing, wide verges are more easily kept than narrow ones. A width of from 2 to 3 ft. is ideal if space and garden lay-out permit. Inner and outer edges should generally be parallel.

Renovation and Widening Often by the end of the summer the edges may become ragged, broken down or bare. Renovation by seeding should be carried out in the late summer, but since good establishment of seed on the edges is difficult, the following procedure should be adopted. Lift the offending turf cleanly to at least 9 or 12 in. in from the edge, and after turning it round relay with the ragged side inwards. The clean-cut inner side now makes the edge. Top-soil should then be used to correct the level of the ragged area, and seed sown. Narrow verges can be widened by this method. After splitting down the centre the turf is turned round, so bringing the inside cut to the position of the new edges. The centre is then filled with soil and sown.

The edges of verges are sometimes supported by concrete or strips of wood. In spite of this, however, there may be some sinking; then it will be necessary to correct the level of the turf from time to time. An uneven verge makes neat mowing impossible.

Turf Under Trees The maintenance of a satisfactory sward under the cover of trees is not easy, and has been mentioned in Chapter Eight.

The grass should always be left rather longer than in the open, and should be swept periodically to clear off leaves and twigs. Mowing may sometimes be rendered difficult by exposed tree roots. The line of large roots can be found by prodding; if the turf is then nicked the chances are that the root can be drawn out. Soil should then be inserted and the turf stamped back.

Moss should be kept down as far as possible by occasional raking while seed renovation may have to be done from time to time. Light fertilizer dressings are desirable; while liming may be necessary, more particularly in industrial areas. During the summer, water artificially to compensate for the water requirements of the tree and the canopy effect of the branches.

In some instances it is necessary to renew turf annually beneath the trees and, returfing is better than reseeding. Certain grass species, such as rough-stalked meadow-grass and wood-meadow grass, are more tolerant of shade conditions than others.

Lawn Tennis Courts The general management of tennis courts should be as laid down for lawns of good quality. It is even more important on such areas that a uniform surface is obtained to ensure accuracy of bounce of the balls. A succulent cover of grass (induced by excessive nitrogenous feeding) should be avoided, since the turf must withstand reasonable wear and tear.

The aim should be to produce a hard weed-free surface somewhat comparable to a cricket wicket, therefore the roller must be used more than suggested for lawns which are purely ornamental. Careful regular mowing should be carried out at a height of cut no keener than $\frac{3}{16}$ in. (gauged as described in Chapter Nine).

By the end of the season wear and tear will have taken its toll, particularly on the base-lines. By this time it is usually too late to renovate with seed and expect a thorough establishment which will resist the rigours of winter and yet be strong enough to stand play early the following season. The question thus arises as to where to obtain suitable turf; imported turf often does not match the remaining sward, and it is also difficult to get a supply of turf that is both weed-free and clean rooted, not fibrous —two important points. The answer is often to take turf from the surrounds of the court (or between courts if there is more than one), and to renovate these areas with seed the following spring or to turf them with imported sods, or to shift the court to the left or right by some seven yards for a season.

Otherwise the autumn routine is the same as for a good lawn, paying particular attention to the control of weeds and earthworms. Finally, a top-dressing should be given using a medium to heavy loam-soil used for the purpose of binding the surface. Sand is normally not suitable for tennis courts, since it is apt to give rise to a crumbly surface.